Writing Skills

Weekly Units

With thanks to Becky Miles, Susan Purcell, and Elaine Wilkinson.

What do you think? How should the story end?

N n
O o
P p

A a
B b
C c
D d

Make up some names and addresses and write them here.

Plan your race and add in some obstacles here.

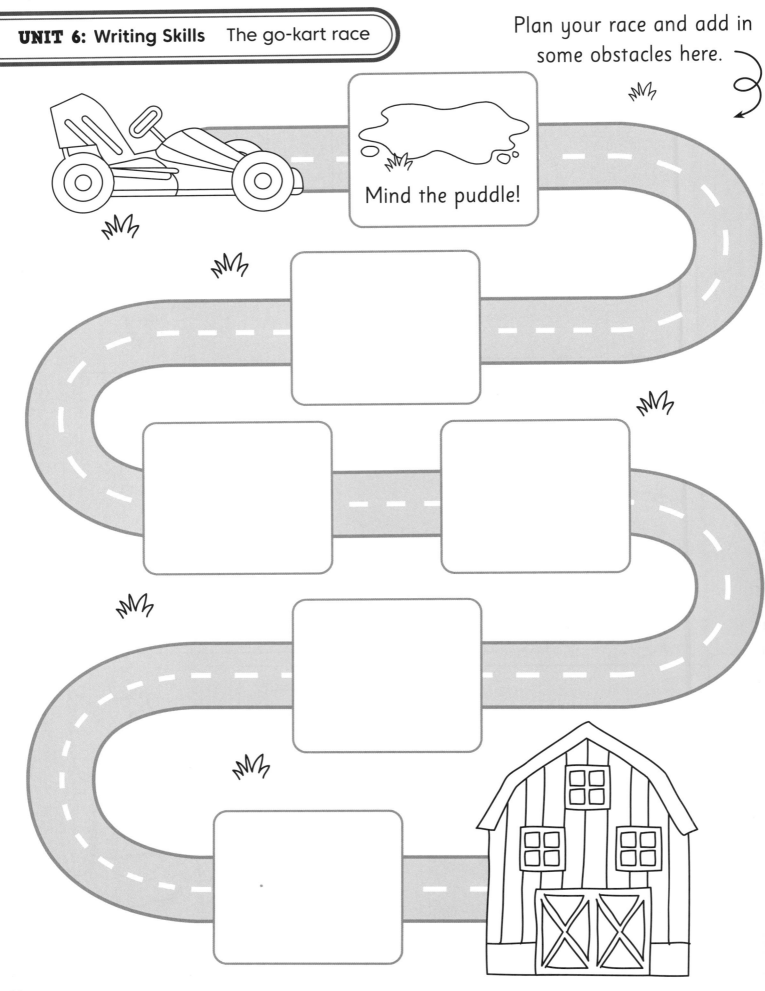

Mind the puddle!

Write about the race here.

....

....

....

....

....

....

....

....

....

....

....

....

....

Monday

Draw your bird picture here.

Copy the rhymes about Snake, Inky, and Bee here.

Try your own rhymes on the next page.

Draw a picture of one
of your animals.

Draw a person wearing a big coat.

Draw the person carrying their coat.

Color the ink splat to match the color you're writing about.

20

Write your color poems here.

To ....

You are invited to

....

Date: ....

Time: ....

Place: ....

From ....

Write about the party here.

Write your cake ingredients here.

With a grown-up's help, turn on the oven to 400°F (200°C) to let it heat up.

Don't forget to leave the cake(s) to cool!

Draw Anansi's route to the melon,
then plan and write your story over the page.

Carry on writing over the page.

Yesteryear

What makes you happy?

What makes you sad?

What will you look like in the future?

....

....

....

....

....

....

....

....

....

....

....

....

....

....

Draw where you will live
in the future.

Carry on writing over the page.

Draw yourself here.

Use this page to write some adjectives.

Write about yourself here.

Draw your monster here.

Write your monster's name here.

C
L
O
U
D
S

Write your rhyming words here.

Try a rhyming sentence here.

Don't forget a story has
a beginning, a middle,
and an end.

Use this page to plan your story.

Carry on writing
over the page.

Don't forget a story has a beginning, a middle, and an end.

Write an animal name and a word that rhymes with it here.

Write what they may say or sound like here.

Write your rhyming sentences here.

Write **how** a person said something here.

Use the words above in sentences here.

Try writing a story using one of your sentences.

Write your dinosaur name here.

Draw your dinosaur here.

Write the name of your sundae here.

Draw your sundae
and add labels
to it here.

List or draw the ingredients.

Write and illustrate
your favorite story here.